Team Spirit

THE CLEVELAND CAVALIERS

BY

MARK STEWART

Content Consultant
Matt Zeysing
Historian and Archivist
The Naismith Memorial Basketball Hall of Fame

NORWOOD HOUSE PRESS
CHICAGO, ILLINOIS

Norwood House Press
P.O. Box 316598
Chicago, Illinois 60631

For information regarding Norwood House Press, please visit our website at:
www.norwoodhousepress.com or call 866-565-2900.

All photos courtesy of Getty Images except the following:
Black Book Partners Archives (6, 28, 36, 40 bottom),
Topps, Inc. (7, 14, 17, 20, 30, 34 left & right, 40 top & bottom left, 43).
Cover photo: David Liam Kyle/Getty Images
Special thanks to Topps, Inc.

Editor: Mike Kennedy
Designer: Ron Jaffe
Project Management: Black Book Partners, LLC.
Research: Joshua Zaffos

Special thanks to Marti Moyer

Library of Congress Cataloging-in-Publication Data

Stewart, Mark, 1960-
  The Cleveland Cavaliers / by Mark Stewart ; content consultant, Matt
Zeysing.
     p. cm. -- (Team spirit)
  Includes bibliographical references and index.
  Summary: "Presents the history and accomplishments of the Cleveland
Cavaliers basketball team. Includes highlights of players, coaches, and
awards, quotes, timelines, maps, glossary and websites"--Provided by
publisher.
  ISBN-13: 978-1-59953-288-2 (library edition : alk. paper)
  ISBN-10: 1-59953-288-3 (library edition : alk. paper) 1. Cleveland
Cavaliers (Basketball team)--History--Juvenile literature. 2.
Basketball--Ohio--Cleveland--History--Juvenile literature. I. Zeysing,
Matt. II. Title.
  GV885.52.C57S74 2009
  796.323'64097713--dc22
                                                      2008044291

COVER PHOTO: The Cavaliers huddle before a 2006–07 game.

Table of Contents

SPORTS WORDS & VOCABULARY WORDS: In this book, you will find many words that are new to you. You may also see familiar words used in new ways. The glossary on page 46 gives the meanings of basketball words, as well as "everyday" words that have special basketball meanings. These words appear in **bold type** throughout the book. The glossary on page 47 gives the meanings of vocabulary words that are not related to basketball. They appear in ***bold italic type*** throughout the book.

BASKETBALL SEASONS: Because each basketball season begins late in one year and ends early in the next, seasons are not named after years. Instead, they are written out as two years separated by a dash, for example 1944–45 or 2005–06.

Meet the Cavaliers

The difference between a winning team and a losing team in the **National Basketball Association (NBA)** often comes down to chemistry. Do the five players on the court make one another better, or do they keep the team from playing its best? Fans of the Cleveland Cavaliers have seen it all. When the "Cavs" play as a tightly knit group, they are hard to beat. When they don't, they have been known to beat themselves.

The Cavaliers have had winning teams made up of well-known stars. They have also had winning teams made up of players who are unknown to most fans. It always seems to come down to how the skills and attitudes of Cleveland's players blend together.

This book tells the story of the Cavaliers. Since joining the NBA in the 1970s, they have played fun, exciting team basketball. Their system has worked whether there have been superstars or **substitutes** on the court. And Cleveland fans believe that can produce a championship.

LeBron James and Daniel Gibson congratulate each other on a good play during the 2006–07 season.

Way Back When

Cleveland, Ohio has been a great basketball town for nearly 100 years. In the 1920s, the city had one of the top **professional** teams in the country. During the 1960s, the Cleveland Pipers won the championship of the American Basketball League, which competed with the older NBA. All along, the city's amateur basketball teams have been among the best in the nation.

In 1970, a businessman named Nick Mileti convinced the NBA that it should start a new team in Cleveland. Mileti owned the Cleveland Arena, which was the home of a popular hockey team. It made good sense to have another sports team in the arena. The Cavaliers were born. They built their team with players who were **overlooked** or unwanted by other teams. They also found great college players.

The Cavaliers struggled to win their first game. In fact, they lost 15 in a row before earning that first victory. Still, the fans came out and supported them. They cheered for young players such as Walt Wesley, John Johnson, and Bingo Smith. In 1971–72 the Cavaliers drafted Austin Carr, a guard who once scored 61 points in a college game. Later they traded for **All-Star** Lenny Wilkens. He taught Cleveland's young stars the tricks he had learned during his many seasons in the NBA.

By the 1975–76 season, coach Bill Fitch had whipped the Cavs into shape. They were one of the toughest defensive teams in the NBA, thanks to three Jims—Brewer, Chones, and Cleamons—and a towering center named Nate Thurmond. The Cavaliers came within two victories of going to the **NBA Finals** that season.

Other stars who wore the Cleveland uniform in the 1970s included Campy Russell, Mike Mitchell, Walt Frazier, and Foots Walker. But it was not until the late 1980s that the Cavaliers

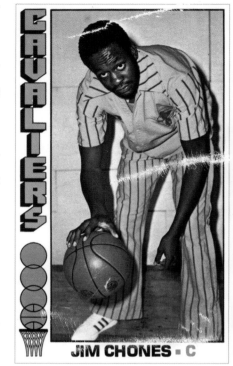

JIM CHONES • C

counted themselves among the NBA's best again. They rebuilt the team into a winner with Mark Price, Brad Daugherty, Larry Nance, Ron Harper, John "Hot Rod" Williams, Danny Ferry, and Craig Ehlo.

Lenny Wilkens returned as Cleveland's coach. He led the Cavaliers to three 50-win seasons. He was followed by Mike Fratello, who also had great success. Both coaches helped make the Cavaliers a fun team to watch.

LEFT: Austin Carr
ABOVE: Jim Chones

Players such as Price, Daugherty, and Nance were very talented and also very unselfish. Every win was a team win. No one cared how many points he scored, as long as the Cavaliers outscored their opponent.

Unfortunately, the team shared the **Central Division** with two *extraordinary* clubs, the Chicago Bulls and Detroit Pistons. Starting in 1987–88, either the Bulls or Pistons went to the NBA Finals for six years in a row. Cleveland often lost to Chicago or Detroit in the **playoffs**.

As their stars aged or got injured, the Cavaliers had a hard time replacing them. The fans started to

realize how lucky they were to have had such a good group for all those years. Many talented players wore the Cleveland uniform in the late 1990s and early 2000s. But the Cavaliers could not find the winning mix. They hoped to change that in the 21st *century*.

LEFT: Mark Price drives for a layup against the Chicago Bulls. He was Cleveland's leader for nine seasons.   **ABOVE**: Larry Nance rises for a jump shot. He combined with Price and Brad Daugherty to give the Cavaliers three top-scorers.

9

The Team Today

In the spring of 2003, Cleveland fans watched breathlessly as the order of **draft picks** was set by the NBA. Why were they so nervous? The best player in the **NBA draft** was 18-year-old LeBron James. He had the talent and drive to boost the Cavs and turn them into a championship *contender*.

The Cavaliers won the NBA's "lottery" and picked James. He was an amazing **all-around** star who proved right away that he could be a force in the league. James seemed to get better with each game. So did the Cavaliers. Within one season, the Cavaliers were winners again.

Cleveland began adding players who would make James better— and who James would make better, too. In his fourth year, the young star led the Cavaliers all the way to the NBA Finals. The city of Cleveland was rocking once more, thanks to the young star everyone called "King James."

LeBron James gets words of encouragement from Anderson Varejao during Cleveland's run to the 2007 NBA Finals.

Home Court

The Cavaliers have played in three famous arenas. Their first, the Cleveland Arena, was the site of the country's first rock and roll concert, in 1952. The show was called the "Moondog Coronation" and featured a variety of bands. In 1974, the team moved into the Richfield Coliseum, which was built a few miles south of the city. It was one of the first arenas to include luxury boxes.

During the 1990s, the city of Cleveland began a big project to rebuild its downtown area. The city built a basketball arena and a football stadium for the Browns of the **National Football League (NFL)**. The Cavaliers moved into their new home in 1994. A *decade* later, it was modernized, with new seats, scoreboards, and video and sound systems.

BY THE NUMBERS

- *The Cavaliers' arena has 20,562 seats for basketball.*
- *There are 92 luxury suites in the team's arena.*
- *As of 2008, the Cavaliers had retired six numbers—7 (Bingo Smith), 22 (Larry Nance), 25 (Mark Price), 34 (Austin Carr), 42 (Nate Thurmond), and 43 (Brad Daugherty).*

LeBron James shoots a free throw during the 2007–08 season. Cleveland's retired numbers hang from the ceiling above him.

Dressed for Success

The team's first *logo* showed a cavalier in a sword fight. What are cavaliers? Cavaliers were Englishmen in the 1600s who fought boldly for honor and country. Today, the team's logo still includes a sword.

The Cavaliers have gone through many uniform changes since they joined the NBA in 1970–71. For more than a decade, their team colors were shades of red and yellow that were known as "wine" and "gold." Cleveland added white in the mid-1970s. During that time, the Cavs changed their lettering style several times, too.

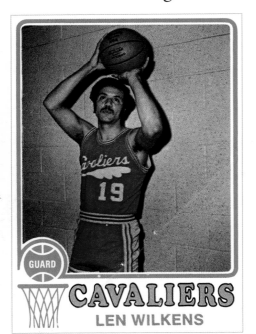

In 1983, the team switched its colors to orange, blue, and white. The uniform read *Cavs* across the front. The *v* in *Cavs* was made to look like a basket and net. In the mid-1990s, the Cavaliers began using light blue as a uniform color. In 2003, they went "back to the future" and switched to their original colors, wine and gold.

Lenny Wilkens models the team's uniform from the early 1970s, which included a feather on the jersey.

14

UNIFORM BASICS

The basketball uniform is very simple. It consists of a roomy top and baggy shorts.

- The top hangs from the shoulders, with big "scoops" for the arms and neck. This style has not changed much over the years.

- Shorts, however, have changed a lot. They used to be very short, so players could move their legs freely. In the last 20 years, shorts have actually gotten longer and much baggier.

Basketball uniforms look the same as they did long ago … until you look very closely. In the old days, the shorts had belts and buckles. The tops were made of a thick cotton called "jersey," which got very heavy when players sweated. Later, uniforms were made of shiny *satin*. They may have looked great, but they did not "breathe." Players got very hot! Today, most uniforms are made of *synthetic* materials that soak up sweat and keep the body cool.

Ben Wallace heads down the court in the team's 2007–08 home uniform.

We Won!

The Cavaliers have had many good teams and good players over the years. Only a few times, however, have they had a team that could challenge for the NBA Championship. Cleveland started the 1975–76 season with a nice mix of players, including Campy Russell, Jim Cleamons, Austin Carr, Bingo Smith, Jim Brewer, Dick Snyder, and Jim Chones. The Cavaliers could shoot, pass, rebound, and play defense. When they struggled to win early in the year, coach Bill Fitch realized they needed something more.

That November, Cleveland traded for Nate Thurmond. He was a big, tough center who would not let anyone near the basket. That allowed his teammates to gamble on defense. If they tried for a steal, they knew Thurmond would be there to back them up. The Cavaliers finished with 49 wins and won the Central Division title.

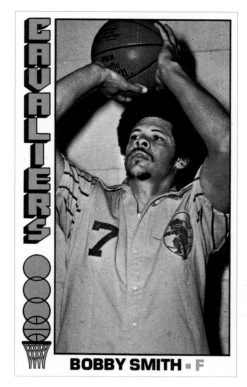

BOBBY SMITH ▪ F

Heading into the playoffs, they thought they were good enough to win it all.

They would have to prove this against the Washington Bullets. The experts looked at Washington's stars—Elvin Hayes, Dave Bing, Phil Chenier, and Wes Unseld—and predicted a wipeout. When the Bullets won Game 1 in Cleveland, it appeared as if the experts might be right.

At the end of Game 2, the Bullets led by one point with the clock winding down. The Cavaliers played great defense and got the ball back with six seconds left. Smith dribbled down the court and made a long jump shot for an incredible 80–79 win. It was the first **postseason** victory in team history. The two teams fought hard and split the next four games.

Game 7 was played in front of the noisiest crowd ever heard at the Richfield Coliseum. More than 21,000 fans squeezed into the building. They saw another close game. Cleveland led 85–83 with less than a minute left. Chenier made a basket for Washington to tie the score. Cleveland struck back. The Cavs won the game with four seconds left

when Snyder drove past Unseld and made a running bank shot high off the backboard.

The "Miracle of Richfield" ended in the next series against the Boston Celtics. Chones injured his foot and could not help Thurmond against Boston's great rebounders. The Celtics won in six games and went on to win the NBA title. To this day, everyone on that Cleveland team believes they missed a great opportunity.

"After we got Nate, I thought we were the best team in the league that year," says Fitch. "If Jim Chones hadn't hurt his foot in between the Washington and Boston series, I knew we would have won the title."

The Cavaliers finally reached the NBA Finals 31 years later. LeBron James led Cleveland into the playoffs, with help from Zydrunas Ilgauskas,

Drew Gooden, and Daniel Gibson. After beating the Washington Wizards in the first round, the Cavaliers **overwhelmed** the New Jersey Nets in the second round.

That set up a series with the Detroit Pistons. One year earlier, the Pistons had beaten the Cavs in the playoffs. They held Cleveland to just 61 points in the last game. The Cavaliers were still **embarrassed** about that loss.

At first, it looked as if the Pistons would win again. They beat Cleveland in the first two games. James had a chance to tie Game 1 with only seconds remaining. Instead, he passed to a teammate who missed a shot. In Game 2, James clanked a shot off the rim that would have won the contest for Cleveland. Over the next four games, however, James was brilliant. The Cavaliers swept all four and made it to the NBA Finals for the first time.

Unfortunately, Cleveland's amazing run ended just short of a championship. Still, Cavaliers fans celebrated the best season in team history. They also knew that James had arrived as a superstar.

LEFT: LeBron James soars above the New Jersey Nets for a basket during the 2007 playoffs.   **ABOVE**: Ira Newble, Zydrunas Ilgauskas, and Drew Gooden celebrate after Cleveland's series win over the Detroit Pistons.

Go-To Guys

To be a true star in the NBA, you need more than a great shot. You have to be a "go-to guy"—someone teammates trust to make the winning play when the seconds are ticking away in a big game. Cavaliers fans have had a lot to cheer about over the years, including these great stars ...

THE PIONEERS

BINGO SMITH   6´ 5″ Guard/Forward

• BORN: 2/26/1946   • PLAYED FOR TEAM: 1970–71 TO 1979–80

No shot was too long for Bingo Smith. In the days before the NBA used the **3-point shot**, Smith often bombed away from 25 or 30 feet. That forced opponents to guard him far from the basket and opened up space for his teammates.

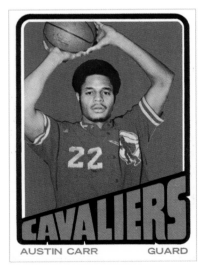

AUSTIN CARR   GUARD

AUSTIN CARR   6´ 4″ Guard

• BORN: 3/10/1948

• PLAYED FOR TEAM: 1971–72 TO 1979–80

Austin Carr was one of the greatest scorers in college basketball history. Leg and foot injuries kept him from being a superstar in the NBA, but he was still one of the top players at his position.

CAMPY RUSSELL   6´ 8˝ Forward

- BORN: 1/12/1952   • PLAYED FOR TEAM: 1974–75 TO 1979–80 & 1984–85

Campy Russell was a talented and popular player who often scored 20 or more points a game. Russell made his one and only trip to the All-Star Game as a member of the Cavs.

CRAIG EHLO   6´ 6˝ Guard

- BORN: 8/11/1961   • PLAYED FOR TEAM: 1986–87 TO 1992–93

Cleveland fans loved Craig Ehlo because he was a great team player. Ehlo often guarded an opponent's top offensive star. He was also a **clutch** outside shooter. His nickname was "Mr. Everything."

BRAD DAUGHERTY   7´ 0˝ Center

- BORN:10/19/1965

- PLAYED FOR TEAM: 1986–87 TO 1993–94

Brad Daugherty was smart and smooth on the court. The Cavaliers used the first pick in the 1986 NBA draft on him. Cleveland fans expected 20 points and 10 rebounds a game from Daugherty, and he usually delivered for them.

MARK PRICE   6´ 0˝ Guard

- BORN: 2/15/1964

- PLAYED FOR TEAM: 1986–87 TO 1994–95

No one in the NBA could out-shoot Mark Price. When he was open, he rarely missed. Price was also one of the best free-throw shooters in league history. He was the first Cavalier to be named First Team **All-NBA**.

LEFT: Austin Carr   **ABOVE**: Brad Daugherty

MODERN STARS

LARRY NANCE
6′ 10″ Forward

- BORN: 2/12/1959 • PLAYED FOR TEAM: 1987–88 TO 1993–94

Larry Nance could do it all on the basketball court. He was a great leaper who loved to dunk. He was also an excellent rebounder and shot-blocker. Nance set team records with seven blocks in a quarter and 11 in a game.

TERRELL BRANDON
5′ 11″ Guard

- BORN: 5/20/1970

- PLAYED FOR TEAM: 1991–92 TO 1996–97

During his six seasons in Cleveland, Terrell Brandon turned into one of the top point guards in the league. He could dribble, pass, score, and play defense. Brandon was also a respected leader on the court and in the community.

ZYDRUNAS ILGAUSKAS 7′ 3″ Center

- BORN: 6/5/1975

- FIRST SEASON WITH TEAM: 1997–98

Zydrunas Ilgauskas began his career as a star in his home country of Lithuania. He continued his great play in the NBA. Ilgauskas was especially good at "cleaning the glass." He led the NBA in **offensive rebounds** in 2004–05.

ANDRE MILLER   6′ 2″ Guard

- BORN: 3/19/1976
- PLAYED FOR TEAM: 1999–00 TO 2001–02

When it comes to finding the open man, few players have ever been as good as Andre Miller. He made the NBA's **All-Rookie** team in 1999–00. Two years later, Miller set a team record for **assists** in a season with 882.

LeBRON JAMES   6′ 8″ Forward

- BORN: 12/30/1984
- FIRST SEASON WITH TEAM: 2003–04

LeBron James went straight from high school to the NBA. Once he turned professional, he had to learn "on the job" what it meant to be a superstar. In his fourth season, James led the Cavaliers to the NBA Finals. A year after that, he was the league scoring champion and **Most Valuable Player (MVP)** of the All-Star Game.

DANIEL GIBSON   6′ 2″ Guard

- BORN: 2/27/1986
- FIRST SEASON WITH TEAM: 2006–07

Daniel Gibson did whatever the Cavs asked of him. During the 2007 playoffs, he came off the bench and was simply spectacular. Gibson always played fearlessly and loved to take the game-winning shot.

LEFT: Terrell Brandon
ABOVE: Daniel Gibson and LeBron James

On the Sidelines

The Cavaliers have had some of the NBA's best coaches over the years. Their first, Bill Fitch, was known for turning bad teams into good ones. He did that with the Cavs. Fitch demanded that his players be in peak condition at all times. This helped them win close games in the final moments, when their opponents were getting tired. In 1976, Fitch brought the Cavs to the **Eastern Conference Finals** for the first time.

Lenny Wilkens played for the Cavaliers in the 1970s and coached them in the 1980s. He convinced a group of great shooters that they could win if they put more energy into defense and rebounding. Wilkens guided Cleveland to the playoffs five times during his seven seasons with the team. In almost any other era, the Cavs might have reached the NBA Finals. But Michael Jordan and the Chicago Bulls almost always stood in their way.

Like Wilkens, Mike Brown got the Cavaliers to believe in the power of defense. Brown had learned a lot about winning as an assistant to Gregg Popovich of the San Antonio Spurs. In his second season, he led Cleveland all the way to the NBA Finals.

Mark Price receives instructions from Lenny Wilkens. He was one of Cleveland's most successful coaches.

One Great Day

When a great player is firing on all cylinders, it is something to behold. A lot of experts wondered just how good LeBron James could be. He had a chance to show them during the 2007 Eastern Conference Finals. The Cavaliers were playing the Detroit Pistons. Detroit had talent and experience. The Pistons specialized in beating teams built around one star player.

Early in the series, the Pistons handled James easily and won the first two games. James did not panic. He improved his play, and the Cavs won the next two games. Even so, many Cleveland fans were *frustrated* with their young star. They thought James had to take control. In Game 5, he did exactly that.

In the fourth quarter, James was unstoppable. He tied the score 91–91 with a tremendous dunk, and the game went into **overtime**. James kept shooting and scoring. He scored all nine of his team's points in the extra period. The Pistons scored nine, too. The two teams had to play a second overtime.

LeBron James slices through the defense for the winning basket
in Game 5 against the Detroit Pistons.

With Cleveland behind 107–104, James hit a fadeaway 3-pointer to tie the score. With two seconds left, he powered to the basket past four Detroit players for a layup. The Cavaliers won the game, 109–107.

"That was the single best game I've ever seen at this level," said Cleveland coach Mike Brown.

Indeed it was. James had scored 29 of the Cavaliers' last 30 points against one of the best defensive teams in the NBA. "Not everybody gets the opportunity to be in a zone like that," James recalled. "I just wanted to will my team to victory and do the best job possible."

"We threw everything we had at him," said Chauncey Billups, the leader of the Pistons. "We just couldn't stop him."

Legend Has It

Which Cavalier once dunked in his own basket?

LEGEND HAS IT that John Warren did. The Cavaliers were still trying for their first victory when they met the Portland Trailblazers early in the 1970–71 season. The Cavs had a chance to win late in the game. Bill Fitch called a timeout and told his players to go for a quick basket. Bobby Lewis scanned the floor for an open teammate. He saw Warren cutting to the basket all alone. Warren caught Lewis's pass and dunked. The crowd was silent. In his excitement, Warren had gotten mixed up and scored a basket for Portland. The Cavs lost 105–103.

ABOVE: John Warren, the Cavalier who scored two points for the wrong team. **RIGHT**: Larry Nance shows off his favorite number.

Who was the fastest Cavalier?

LEGEND HAS IT that Larry Nance was. Nance was fascinated by drag racing. He owned a drag racer and ran a racing team while he was with the Cavaliers. His car was number 22—the same number he wore for Cleveland. Nance's contract did not allow him to drive in drag races. As soon as Nance retired from basketball, he became a full-time owner and driver.

Who was Cleveland's toughest coach?

LEGEND HAS IT that Bill Fitch was. Before he started coaching, Fitch was a *drill sergeant* for the U.S. Marines. He believed that training camp was a time for players to get in shape. One year, he made the Cavs practice morning and afternoon for 21 days in a row. Later, when Fitch coached the Boston Celtics, All-Star Larry Bird said that he was the person who taught him about the rewards of hard work.

It Really Happened

In January of 1980, the Cavaliers and Los Angeles Lakers were two teams headed in different directions. Cleveland would finish with just 37 wins. Los Angeles was on its way to the NBA Championship.

Still, it was a big night when the Lakers visited Richfield Coliseum that season. More than 13,000 fans showed up for the

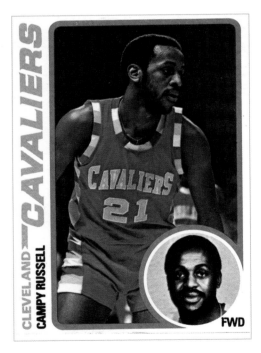

game. They were eager to watch Magic Johnson, Kareem Abdul-Jabbar, and the rest of the star-studded Los Angeles team. The Cavaliers had a mix of young and older players. Their top scorers were young forwards Mike Mitchell and Campy Russell. The team leaders were **veterans** Randy Smith and Dave Robisch.

The Lakers held a 114–112 lead with less than one minute to go. Mitchell swished a short jump shot to tie the game and send it into overtime. Each team scored 12 points in the extra period. With the score tied 126–126, the Lakers and Cavs had to play another overtime.

At this point, winning became a matter of pride. The players were exhausted, but they continued to give everything they had. The Cavaliers led 136–134 with 33 seconds left. The Lakers got the ball to Abdul-Jabbar, and Cleveland fouled him. He made two free throws to send the game into a third overtime.

Once again, the Cavaliers managed to build a two-point lead. Once again, the Lakers' big center was too much to handle. Abdul-Jabbar made a basket with 19 seconds left to tie the game at 144–144 and force a fourth overtime!

Cleveland fans breathed a sigh of relief when Abdul-Jabbar was whistled for his sixth foul with 18 seconds left in the fourth extra period. The Lakers led 153–152, but Cleveland now had the ball. Mitchell drove to the basket with two seconds left and was hit on the arm. He made two free throws to give the Cavaliers a 154–153 victory.

Three Cavaliers—Mitchell, Robisch, and Smith—scored 30 or more points in the game. That was a team record. The Lakers also set a record that night. At the time, 153 points were the most ever scored by a losing team.

LEFT: Campy Russell
ABOVE: Mike Mitchell

Team Spirit

The fans that pack the arena for Cavaliers games come from the city, the country, and the suburbs. They have two things in common. First, they love the Cavs. Second, they expect to be entertained non-stop from the moment they take their seats.

The Cavaliers do a good job of this while they are on the court. During timeouts and between periods, the Cleveland Cavalier Girls take center stage. They are a dance team that performs in the arena. They appear at schools and charity events all over Ohio, too. Cleveland fans also cheer for a group of acrobatic dancers called the Scream Team.

Music is also an important part of game night in the Cavaliers' arena. That is because Cleveland takes its rock music seriously. The Rock and Roll *Hall of Fame* is nearby. Sometimes famous musicians are in the crowd to watch LeBron James and the Cavs play. The team's *mascot*, Moondog, is named after Alan "Moondog" Freed, a famous Cleveland disc jockey from the 1950s.

Moondog flies through the air for a dunk.

Timeline

The basketball season is played from October through June. That means each season takes place at the end of one year and the beginning of the next. In this timeline, the accomplishments of the Cavaliers are shown by season.

1970–71
The Cavaliers play their first season.

1986–87
Brad Daugherty, Ron Harper, and John Williams are named to the All-Rookie team.

1972–73
Dwight Davis is named to the NBA All-Rookie Team.

1980–81
The All-Star Game is played in Cleveland.

1988–89
Larry Nance makes the NBA **All-Defensive Team**.

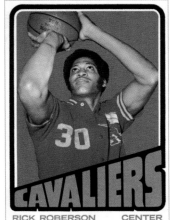

RICK ROBERSON   CENTER

Rick Roberson, a star for the Cavs in their early days.

John "Hot Rod" Williams

JOHN WILLIAMS

Steve
Kerr

Andre
Miller

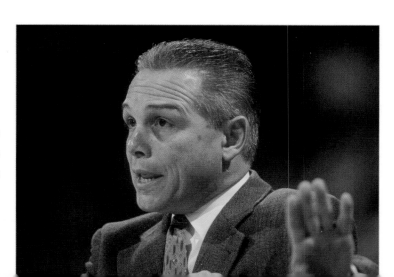

2007–08
Daniel Gibson is the top
scorer in the All-Star
Rookie Challenge Game.

1989–90
Steve Kerr is the NBA's
top 3-point shooter.

2001–02
Andre Miller leads
the league in assists.

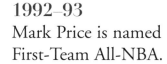

1992–93
Mark Price is named
First-Team All-NBA.

1997–98
The team has its 7th
winning season in a row.

2006–07
The Cavaliers reach
the NBA Finals for
the first time.

Mike Fratello, the
coach of the Cavs
for six seasons
during the 1990s.

Fun Facts

STAR POWER

In 1972, Butch Beard and John Johnson were chosen to play in the All-Star Game. The next time two or more Cavs played in the game was  1989. Mark Price, Brad Daugherty, and Larry Nance made the team that year.

HAIR TODAY

Hairstyles come and go, but two Cavaliers will always be remembered for their "big" hair. In the 1970s, Bingo Smith had one of the NBA's most magnificent afros. In recent years, Anderson Varejao had a head-turning head of hair.

FOUNTAIN OF YOUTH

In 2004, 19-year-old LeBron James became the youngest player to win NBA **Rookie of the Year**. In 2005, he became the youngest player to record a **triple-double**. In 2006, James was the youngest player to be voted MVP of the All-Star Game.

NO ORDINARY JOE

Since 1970, Cleveland fans have been listening to Joe Tait call Cavaliers games. He took two years off in the 1980s. But as the 2008–09 season began, Tait was back and starting his 36th year.

THAT 70s SHOW

In 1970–71, Walt Wesley became the first Cavalier to score 50 points in a game. In 1971–72, Rick Roberson set team records with 25 rebounds in a game and 12.7 rebounds per game for a season.

CAR TALK

Brad Daugherty's greatest sports hero was race-car driver Richard Petty. Daugherty chose number 43 because it was Petty's car number. Daugherty later became an announcer on racing broadcasts.

LEFT: Bingo Smith shows off his famous afro.
ABOVE: Joe Tait, Cleveland's beloved broadcaster.

Talking Hoops

"We had some special and talented teams here in Cleveland, and we knew we could compete with anyone in the league."
—*Mark Price, on the Cavaliers of the late 1980s and early 1990s*

"One of the main goals outside of winning a championship is to be an All-Star, or to play at that level. I definitely strived to achieve that every year. And I felt proud to make the team."
—*Austin Carr, on making the All-Star team in 1974*

"We were always winning and playing well—so well that no one could stop us when we were healthy."
—*Larry Nance, on the Cavaliers at their best*

ABOVE: Austin Carr   **RIGHT**: LeBron James

"Sometimes the coaches tell me to be selfish, but my game won't let me be selfish."

—*LeBron James, on being a team player*

"Guys had strong ties to each other—we lived by each other, hung out together, went to dinner together. And because of the bond, guys made their home in Cleveland. That was special."

—*Bingo Smith, on the Cavaliers of the mid-1970s*

"That was one special year. We put aside our individual desires and bought into the team concept. I've never felt closer to a group of guys than during that season."

—*Nate Thurmond, on the 1975–76 Cavaliers*

For the Record

T he great Cavaliers teams and players have left their marks on the record books. These are the "best of the best" …

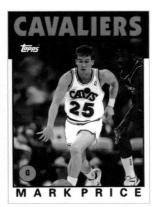

Mark Price

CAVALIERS AWARD WINNERS

WINNER	AWARD	SEASON
Bill Fitch	Coach of the Year	1975–76
Mark Price	3-Point Shootout Champion	1992–93
Mark Price	3-Point Shootout Champion	1993–94
LeBron James	Rookie of the Year	2003–04
LeBron James	All-Star Game MVP	2005–06
LeBron James	All-Star Game MVP	2007–08

CAVALIERS ACHIEVEMENTS

ACHIEVEMENT	SEASON
Central Division Champions	1975–76
Eastern Conference Champions	2006–07

LeBron James

RIGHT: Bill Fitch
FAR RIGHT: LeBron James and the Cavs celebrate after winning the 2007 Eastern Conference Championship.

Pinpoints

The history of a basketball team is made up of many smaller stories. These stories take place all over the map—not just in the city a team calls "home." Match the push-pins on these maps to the Team Facts and you will begin to see the story of the Cavaliers unfold!

TEAM FACTS

1 Cleveland, Ohio—*The Cavaliers have played here since 1970–71.*

2 Black Mountain, North Carolina—*Brad Daugherty was born here.*

3 Washington, D.C.—*Austin Carr was born here.*

4 Fort Myers, Florida—*Walt Wesley was born here.*

5 Sorrento, Louisiana—*John Williams was born here.*

6 Jackson, Tennessee—*Campy Russell was born here.*

7 Davenport, Iowa—*Bill Fitch was born here.*

8 Racine, Wisconsin—*Jim Chones was born here.*

9 Bartlesville, Oklahoma—*Mark Price was born here.*

10 Oakland, California—*Drew Gooden was born here.*

11 Kaunas, Lithuania—*Zydrunas Ilgauskas was born here.*

12 Santa Teresa, Brazil—*Anderson Varejao was born here.*

Zydrunas Ilgauskas

43

Play Ball

Basketball is a sport played by two teams of five players. NBA games have four 12-minute quarters—48 minutes in all—and the team that scores the most points when time has run out is the winner. Most baskets count for two points. Players who make shots from beyond the three-point line receive an extra point. Baskets made from the free-throw line count for one point. Free throws are penalty shots awarded to a team, usually after an opponent has committed a foul. A foul is called when one player makes hard contact with another.

Players can move around all they want, but the player with the ball cannot. He must bounce the ball with one hand or the other (but never both) in order to go from one part of the court to another. As long as he keeps "dribbling," he can keep moving.

In the NBA, teams must attempt a shot every 24 seconds, so there is little time to waste. The job of the defense is to make it as difficult as possible to take a good shot—and to grab the ball if the other team shoots and misses.

This may sound simple, but anyone who has played the game knows that basketball can be very complicated. Every player on the court has a job to do. Different players have different strengths and weaknesses. The coach must mix these players in just the right way, and teach them to work together as one.

The more you play and watch basketball, the more "little things" you are likely to notice. The next time you are at a game, look for these plays:

PLAY LIST

ALLEY-OOP—A play where the passer throws the ball just to the side of the rim—so a teammate can catch it and dunk in one motion.

BACK-DOOR PLAY—A play where the passer waits for his teammate to fake the defender away from the basket—then throws him the ball when he cuts back toward the basket.

KICK-OUT—A play where the ball-handler waits for the defense to surround him—then quickly passes to a teammate who is open for an outside shot. The ball is not really kicked in this play; the term comes from the action of pinball machines.

NO-LOOK PASS—A play where the passer fools a defender (with his eyes) into covering one teammate—then suddenly passes to another without looking.

PICK-AND-ROLL—A play where one teammate blocks or "picks off" another's defender with his body—then cuts to the basket for a pass in the confusion.

Glossary

BASKETBALL WORDS TO KNOW

3-POINT SHOT—A basket made from behind the 3-point line.

ALL-AROUND—Good at all parts of the game.

ALL-DEFENSIVE TEAM—An honor given at the end of each season to the NBA's best defensive players at each position.

ALL-NBA—An honor given at the end of the season to the NBA's best players at each position.

ALL-ROOKIE—An honor given at the end of the season to the NBA's best first-year players at each position.

ALL-STAR—A player selected to play in the annual All-Star Game.

ASSISTS—Passes that lead to successful shots.

CENTRAL DIVISION—A group of teams that plays in the central part of the country.

CLUTCH—Able to perform well under pressure.

DRAFT PICKS—College players selected or "drafted" by NBA teams each summer.

EASTERN CONFERENCE FINALS—The playoff series that determines which team from the East will play the best team from the West for the NBA Championship.

MOST VALUABLE PLAYER (MVP)—The award given each year to the league's best player; also given to the best player in the league finals and All-Star Game.

NATIONAL BASKETBALL ASSOCIATION (NBA)—The professional league that has been operating since 1946–47.

NATIONAL FOOTBALL LEAGUE (NFL)—The league that started in 1920 and is still operating today.

NBA DRAFT—The annual meeting where teams pick from a group of the best college players.

NBA FINALS—The playoff series that decides the champion of the league.

OFFENSIVE REBOUNDS—Rebounds of shots missed by teammates.

OVERTIME—The extra period played when a game is tied after 48 minutes.

PLAYOFFS—The games played after the season to determine the league champion.

POSTSEASON—Another term for playoffs.

PROFESSIONAL—A player or team that plays a sport for money. College players are not paid, so they are considered "amateurs."

ROOKIE OF THE YEAR—The annual award given to the league's best first-year player.

SUBSTITUTES—Players who begin most games on the bench.

TRIPLE-DOUBLE—A game in which a player records double-figures in three different statistical categories.

VETERANS—Players with great experience.

OTHER WORDS TO KNOW

CENTURY—A period of 100 years.

CONTENDER—A team or person that competes for a championship.

DECADE—A period of 10 years; also specific periods, such as the 1950s.

DRILL SERGEANT—A military officer in charge of training new soldiers.

EMBARRASSED—Felt dismayed or awkward.

EXTRAORDINARY—Unusual, or unusually talented.

FRUSTRATED—Disappointed and puzzled.

HALL OF FAME—A museum where people from a particular sport or field of expertise are honored.

LOGO—A symbol or design that represents a company or team.

MASCOT—An animal or person believed to bring a group good luck.

OVERLOOKED—Ignored or not noticed.

OVERWHELMED—Defeated by a greater force.

SYNTHETIC—Made in a laboratory, not in nature.

SATIN—A smooth, shiny fabric.

SYSTEM—An organized plan for success.

Places to Go

ON THE ROAD

CLEVELAND CAVALIERS
One Center Court
Cleveland, Ohio 44115
(216) 420-2000

NAISMITH MEMORIAL BASKETBALL HALL OF FAME
1000 West Columbus Avenue
Springfield, Massachusetts 01105
(877) 4HOOPLA

ON THE WEB

THE NATIONAL BASKETBALL ASSOCIATION   www.nba.com
  • *Learn more about the league's teams, players, and history*

THE CLEVELAND CAVALIERS   www.nba.com/cavaliers
  • *Learn more about the Cavaliers*

THE BASKETBALL HALL OF FAME   www.hoophall.com
  • *Learn more about history's greatest players*

ON THE BOOKSHELF

To learn more about the sport of basketball, look for these books at your library or bookstore:

  • Hareas, John. *Basketball.* New York, New York: DK, 2005.

  • Hughes, Morgan. *Basketball.* Vero Beach, Florida: Rourke Publishing, 2005.

  • Thomas, Keltie. *How Basketball Works.* Berkeley, California: Maple Tree Press, distributed through Publishers Group West, 2005.

Index

The Team

MARK STEWART has written more than 20 books on basketball, and over 100 sports books for kids. He grew up in New York City during the 1960s rooting for the Knicks and Nets, and now takes his two daughters, Mariah and Rachel, to watch them play. Mark comes from a family of writers. His grandfather was Sunday Editor of *The New York Times* and his mother was Articles Editor of *The Ladies Home Journal* and *McCall's*. Mark has profiled hundreds of athletes over the last 20 years. He has also written several books about his native New York, and New Jersey, his home today. Mark is a graduate of Duke University, with a degree in history. He lives with his daughters and wife, Sarah, overlooking Sandy Hook, New Jersey.

MATT ZEYSING is the resident historian at the Basketball Hall of Fame in Springfield, Massachusetts. His research interests include the origins of the game of basketball, the development of professional basketball in the first half of the twentieth century, and the culture and meaning of basketball in American society.